The Corporate Manslaughter and Corporate Homicide Act 2007

Lucas Ullrich

The Corporate Manslaughter and Corporate Homicide Act 2007

In Comparison with German Law

VDM Verlag Dr. Müller

Imprint

Bibliographic information by the German National Library: The German National Library lists this publication at the German National Bibliography; detailed bibliographic information is available on the Internet at http://dnb.d-nb.de.

Cover image: www.purestockx.com

Publisher:
VDM Verlag Dr. Müller Aktiengesellschaft & Co. KG, Dudweiler Landstr. 125 a, 66123 Saarbrücken, Germany,
Phone +49 681 9100-698, Fax +49 681 9100-988,
Email: info@vdm-verlag.de

Produced in USA and UK by:
Lightning Source Inc., La Vergne, Tennessee, USA
Lightning Source UK Ltd., Milton Keynes, UK
BookSurge LLC, 5341 Dorchester Road, Suite 16, North Charleston, SC 29418, USA

ISBN: 978-3-8364-9625-4

Content

Abbreviations

BGB	Bürgerliches Gesetzbuch
CPS	Crown Prosecution Service
Crim.L.F.	Criminal Law Forum
Crim.L.R.	The Criminal Law Review
HSE	Health and Safety Executive
HSWA	Health and Safety at Work Act 1974
HSMO	Health Services Material Officer
ILJ	Industrial law Journal
JotP	Justice of the Peace
NJW	Neue Juristische Wochenschrift
NLJ	New Law Journal
ORR	Office of Rail Regulation
OWiG	Ordnungswidrigkeitengesetz
StGB	Strafgesetzbuch

1.0 Introduction

The corporate entity as a business form dates back to almost ancient times. The first corporations arose during the thirteenth century as entities to manage church property. Two centuries later the first trade organisations were incorporated. England as the world's most progressive country at that time took a leading role in the evolution of corporations.[1]

Today, the corporation is one of the most favoured forms of business entities. Their activities have tremendous impact on the society and a society's legal code must consequently attempt to provide a framework for lawfulness and unlawfulness of corporate actions.[2] Problems occur when corporate actions allegedly kill people and the criminal law must answer with whom liability should rest. Can corporations kill, or only their employees?[3]

Despite the global existence of corporations, there is no global or homogeneous approach to this question. Countries have taken different legal approaches to handle corporate liability for crimes.[4] While the Anglo-American countries have a lot of experience in the criminal prosecution of corporations, some European countries like Sweden completely reject the idea of criminal punishment for corporations.[5] However, many countries that formerly also rejected corporate liability at criminal law, have adopted it into their legal codes over the last years.[6]

Recently the British debate on corporate liability has been renewed when the Corporate Manslaughter and Corporate Homicide Act was finally given royal assent.[7] This act creates the criminal offence of manslaughter in the corporate sphere. The Corporate Manslaughter and Corporate Homicide act also

---

[1] Keenan, English Law, p. 246.
[2] Clarkson, Corporate Culpability, p. 2.
[3] Eisenberg, Corporations and other Business Organizations, p. 100.
[4] Eidam, Straftäter Unternehmen, p. 30.
[5] Senge / Rogall, OWiG, 3rd ed., §30, p.544, para. 241.
[6] For example France did this in 1994. Haeusermann, Der Verband als Straftäter, p. 45.
[7] Home Office, Corporate Manslaughter Act Explanatory Notes, p.1.

constitutes the main approach to this thesis and to the questions it attempts to answer: Why was it necessary to create a new offence? How will the Act affect the British solution to corporate criminality in the sphere of manslaughter? And might such a legal change be necessary in the German legal system? Consequently this paper is only concerned with the *criminal* liability of corporations and does not touch upon the civil liability (although reference is made to such legislation). Furthermore, it does not discuss the various means of individual liability according to German law or British law.

The first main part discusses the development of corporate liability in the British legal system under the context of homicides by negligence and establishes the status quo of corporate manslaughter (part 2.0). Subsequently it focuses on the necessity of the Corporate Manslaughter and Corporate Homicide Act 2007 and the effects this Act might have on the current situation (part 3.0). Lastly, it concentrates on the German solution to corporate criminality in order to determine if the German penal code lacks the offence of corporate manslaughter (part 4.0 and 5.0).

2.0 The History of Corporate Manslaughter in the UK

2.1 Introduction

Common Law has always been known for its flexibility to adapt to new situations. Consequently, the rise of corporations was accompanied by a gradual acceptance of corporate liability. However, this acceptance was more a step-by-step process than a one-time event.

This part demonstrates that fatalities can be a result of corporate decisions in the sense that one can reasonably refer to a killing as corporate manslaughter. Further, it shows how the current British law has been treating these homicides. Lastly, the key obstacles, which have prevented many companies from being prosecuted for manslaughter, are identified and analyzed. The analysis shows that the status quo is inadequate to deal with corporate liability regarding manslaughter and concludes that a legal change was necessary.

2.2 Failed Prosecutions over the last three Decades

> *"[The] Government is committed to delivering safe and secure communities [...]. A fundamental part of this is providing offences that are clear and effective. The current laws on corporate manslaughter are neither [...]."*[8]

2.2.1 Herald of Free Enterprise Capsize

In 1987, 193 people died when the Herald of Free Enterprise capsized shortly after it left the harbour of Zebrugge, Belgium.[9] The crew member responsible for closing the bow doors was asleep in his cabin.[10] The company did not maintain a sufficient system of safety to ensure that the bow doors were closed

---

[8] Home Office, Corporate Manslaughter Draft Bill, p. 5.
[9] Wells, Crim.L.F. 1995, p. 62.
[10] Ibid.

before setting to sail. Water drained into the car deck and the ship sank within minutes. The disaster led to a public inquiry[11] in which Lord Justice Sheen identified a "disease of sloppiness" on every level of the company hierarchy[12]. Only on the basis of his findings and after a judicial review of that report the prosecution decided to bring charges for manslaughter against P&O European Ferries. However, the trial did not stand a chance because the judge was not convinced that the prosecutors could link actions which led to the catastrophic events to one employee senior enough to represent the company.

2.2.2 Southall Train Crash

First Great Western Trains was prosecuted for manslaughter after one of their trains collided with a freight train leaving its depot, in 1997.[13] In the tragic accident seven people were killed and another 139 people were severely injured.[14] The driver admitted being distracted and having over-looked a red signal, but the train was knowingly operated by the company with faulty equipment, a switched-off train protection system, and a driver who lacked training in the latter.[15] The company was fined £1.5 million for a violation of the Health and Safety at Work Act[16], but all manslaughter charges had to be dropped because the prosecution could not link the company's managing director for safety with a criminal act leading to the accident.[17]

2.2.3 Ladbroke Grove and Other Train Crashes

Another 31 people were killed and more than 200 people were injured when a Great Western train collided head-on with a multiple unit train operated by Thames Trains in 1999.[18] A public inquiry report by Lord Cullen came to the conclusion that the Thames Trains driver failed to stop at a red signal, but also highlighted the corporate guilt of two companies: Network Rail, responsible for

---

[11] MV Herald of Free Enterprise – Report of the Court No. 8074, by Lord Justice Sheen.
[12] Ibid, quoted in R. v. H.M. Coroner for East Kent 88 Crim. App. at 16.
[13] HSE, Southall Inquiry, p. 93, para. 8.5.
[14] Ibid, p. 17, para. 2.1.
[15] Ibid, p. 88, para. 7.19.
[16] Ibid, p. 94, para. 8.9. Hereinafter HSWA.
[17] Ibid, p. 94 para. 8.8. Also, CPS, Press Release, 2nd July 1999.
[18] HSE, Ladbroke Inquiry, p. 7, para. 2.1.

rail track maintenance, failed to address complaints from drivers about the bad visibility of the signal in question, and Thames Trains for their inadequate training procedures.[19] Both companies were fined for a violation of the Health and Safety at Work Act, but no charges for manslaughter were brought against them because of insufficient evidence to identify an individual within the companies.[20]

Two similar accidents, commonly known as the Hatfield and Potters Bar rail crashes, followed in 2000 and 2002 respectively.[21] The reason that led to the death of eleven people in those crashes can be expressed by the term maintenance deficiencies on the part of the responsible companies. Again, the CPS was not able to prosecute for manslaughter because they could not establish that a directing mind of the company was culpable of a criminal act. [22]

2.2.4 Similarities of all Incidents and the Need for Change

All of the above-named incidents have several facts in common. First, they all involve fatal accidents in which guilt often attached to individuals although the underlying causes were really corporate actions and decisions.[23] This indicates that punishment of the company instead of an individual appears to be more appropriate.[24] Second, the companies alleged to be negligent were either not prosecuted for manslaughter, or the charges for manslaughter were dismissed or dropped because a conviction seemed unlikely. Last, all prosecutions were unsuccessful for the very same reason: The prosecution's burden to prove that one of the indicted companies' directing minds was culpable of manslaughter.[25] This essential requirement coupled with other legal contingencies has created a high bar to successful corporate manslaughter prosecution.

---

[19] Ibid, pp.138, paras. 7.114 – 7.118.
[20] CPS Press Release, 6th December 2005.
[21] For a general overview see HSE "Potters Bar Inquiry" and HSE "Hatfield Inquiry".
[22] CPS Press Release, 6th September 2005 and 17th October 2005.
[23] Herring, Criminal Law, p. 120.
[24] Ibid.
[25] Home Office, Corporate Manslaughter Draft Bill, p. 8, para. 8.

When the Home Secretary admitted in its foreword to the Draft Bill for Reform that the current laws on corporate manslaughter are neither clear nor effective, he referred to exactly this legal difficulty.[26] But the government was only half-way right. Numerous failed prosecutions over the past two decades show that the laws on corporate manslaughter are truly ineffective. In fact, there is no offence called corporate manslaughter to begin with. Instead, corporate liability for such crimes has been established via the common law principles of manslaughter.[27]

2.3 Manslaughter at Common Law

A corporation cannot be created to commit a crime because such a purpose would already make the organisation unlawful in itself[28]. Yet it is an inevitable truth that corporate actions can lead and have led to the death of human persons as many incidents over the last years have shown. As the British law does not provide a corporate offence for manslaughter yet, it is necessary to establish how workplace or industry-related homicides have been treated by the legal code first.

2.3.1 Homicides

Common law distinguishes three different serious offences against a person: Murder, Voluntary Manslaughter, and Involuntary Manslaughter.[29] Murder and Voluntary Manslaughter, being a diminished form of Murder, both require an intent to cause death or severe bodily harm that could possibly lead to death[30]. In cases of voluntary manslaughter the causation of death or bodily harm was still intentional, but is mitigated by extenuating circumstances, such as provocation.[31] Involuntary manslaughter by contrast seeks to punish killings in

---

[26] Home Office, Corporate Manslaughter Draft Bill, p. 4.
[27] Ashworth, Principles of Criminal Law, p. 114.
[28] Ultra Vires means it is beyond its powers to commit a crime. Keenan, English Law, p. 308.
[29] Keenan, English Law, p. 685.
[30] Herring, Criminal Law, p. 89
[31] Ibid, p. 203.

which the offender lacks the intention to kill, but death cannot be said to have been accidental.[32]-

A corporation cannot be liable for the acts of its employees if they were motivated by personal reasons and the corporation could not have had knowledge of the latter.[33] They acted beyond their authority. In the afore-mentioned incidents however, those agents have acted with the corporation's consent and have failed to address their duties as part of the corporate body. Thus, for crimes like the afore-mentioned incidents in which the defendant was obliged to ensure the safety of the deceased, the law foresees the category of involuntary manslaughter by gross negligence. Gross Negligence Manslaughter requires the prosecution to prove that the defendant is in breach of a duty of care owed to the victim and that this breach was the proximate cause of the victim's death. Finally, it must be shown that the defendant's conduct was gross to the extent of a criminal offence.[34]

The above-mentioned requirements incorporate the necessary misconduct to be guilty of an offence: the guilty act also known as actus reus. However, English law provides a notion that such an act makes a person only guilty if his mind is also guilty[35]; *actus non facit reum nisi mens sit rea.*

A person can be guilty of some offences just by fulfilling the requirements of the actus reus, in these cases liability attaches to the offender on a strict basis.[36] But for most serious offences like involuntary manslaughter the prosecution also needs to prove a culpable state of mind, so-called mens rea. The latter is also referred to as the mental element that needs to accompany every criminal offence.[37] Hence, it is the decisive factor used to classify a killing as murder,

---

[32] Ashworth, Principles of Criminal Law, p. 287.
[33] Keenan, Company Law, p. 91
[34] The test for gross negligence manslaughter was established in R. v. Adomako [1994] 3 All ER 79.
   Its application to corporate defendants was established in Attorney General's Reference (No. 2 of 1999).
   Also see, Ashworth, Principles of Criminal Law, p. 292.
[35] Keenan, English Law, p. 677.
[36] Ibid.
[37] Ibid.

voluntary or involuntary manslaughter by attributing an element of mental guilt to the offender.

2.3.2 Corporate Mens Rea

While it is comparatively easy to identify the conduct and the state of mind for an offence in a natural person, this process is more complex for corporations. A corporation is by definition a legal entity.[38] Like a natural personality attaches to individuals, corporate personality attaches to corporations. This corporate personality exists independently from the shareholders and the management.[39] Further, a corporation cannot act, or for the purpose of omissions it cannot omit to act, on its own.[40] But corporate actions and personalities are exercised and expressed by human beings. Those persons do not necessarily have to be the founders of the corporation, but can also be employees or persons performing services for the company. Therefore the employees' actions and minds have to be imputed to the corporation.[41] Common law has developed two theories to this process of imputation.

2.4 Corporate Criminality

Although, in earlier times corporations were believed to not be able to commit an offence because of their artificiality[42], they were gradually held responsible for their actions. Today, a corporation can commit almost any crime according to British law, with the exception of murder because life sentence is the mandatory penalty.[43]

---

[38] Eisenberg, Corporations and other Business Organizations, p. 100.
[39] Ashworth, Criminal Law, p. 113.
[40] Clarkson, Corporate Culpability, p. 3. However, the Australian government introduced a system of corporate mens rea based on corporate culture and policies. See, Wells, Crim.L.R. 1996, p. 553.
[41] Other approaches to corporate liability include aggregation, corporate mens rea and reactive corporate fault. For a detailed overview see Clarkson, Corporate Culpability.
[42] Ackermann, Die juristische Person, p.88.
Lord Thurlow: "It has no soul to damn and no body to kick".
[43] Wells, Crim.L.F. 1995, pp. 56.

2.4.1 Strict and Vicarious Liability

When liability is strict, it attaches to the offender directly. A corporation can be liable regardless of mens rea [44] At criminal law one cannot be liable for the acts of another, thus criminal law is only concerned with individual liability. But for a variety of reasons courts have extended the concept of vicarious liability from the law of tort to criminal law.[45] Vicarious liability renders employers liable for the actions of their employees as long as they have acted within the scope of their employment.[46] But vicarious liability is considered to be too broad for the offence of manslaughter and thus cannot be applied.[47]

The artificiality of corporations and the nature of mens rea coupled with the preclusion of vicarious liability given, it is not surprising that the courts were reluctant to accept the idea that a corporation can be charged with homicide. The first reported case of corporate manslaughter[48] in the UK confirms this view. The case arose after a mining company erected an electric fence to secure their premises and a worker was killed because he stumbled against it. The trial judge held that a company could not be indicted for an offence.[49]

2.4.2 The Identification Doctrine

It was not until 1957, when Lord Denning in H. L. Bolton (Engineering) Ltd. v. T. J. Graham & Sons Ltd. gave rise for what should be known as the identification doctrine.[50] By comparing a corporation to a human being with a brain that controls its actions and a body that executes these actions, he adopted the view that a corporation can only act through its agents and that their minds must be identified with the mind of the corporation.[51] However, he also indicated that not every employee's action and thought are identical with the company, for

---

[44] Ashworth, Principles of Criminal Law, p. 115.
[45] Ibid, p. 116.
[46] Wells, Crim.L.F. 1995, p. 57.
[47] Clarkson, Corporate Culpability, pp. 8-9.
[48] R. v. Cory Bros. [1927].
[49] Wells, Crim.L.F. 1995, pp. 55.
[50] H. L. Bolton (Engineering) Ltd v. T. J. Graham & Sons Ltd. [1956].
[51] Wells, Crim.L.F. 1995, p. 59

example if the employee lacks decisive power.[52] This distinction between agents controlling the company and pure servants also constitutes the main difference to vicarious liability, which renders a company *fully* liable for the actions of its employees. The principle of identification could not overcome the necessity of proving mens rea in general though, but shifted it from the company to an individual.[53]

2.4.3 The Directing Mind Principle

Lord Denning's vivid expression was also referred to in Tesco Supermarkets v Nattrass, a case which could hardly be any further from manslaughter, but became the principal for any offences requiring manslaughter.[54] Tesco was fined for a violation of the Trade Descriptions Act, after a shop manager failed to realize that a product, at this point in time sold and advertised at a special offer price, was out of stock and the ordinary version was sold instead, but still advertised at the special price. As a defence Tesco claimed that another person, the shop manager, was at fault and that they had exercised all due diligence to avoid this violation.[55] Although the court agreed that Tesco had exercised all due diligence, they held that the shop manager was "not another person".[56]

Tesco appealed this decision. The House of Lords applied Denning's identification principle and seized the opportunity to clarify its meaning. If a person is supposed to be identified with the company, it is not sufficient that this person exercises some managerial power or brain-related work, but he or she must have *controlling* influence over the company's actions.[57] According to this idea the shop manager did not qualify to represent the company and, thus, had to be "another person".[58] The court took up Denning's expression of the "directing mind" to distinguish the shop manager from the company, which

---

[52] Ibid.
[53] Ibid, p. 58.
[54] Tesco Supermarkets Ltd. v. Nattrass [1972].
[55] Wells, Crim.L.F. 1995, p. 59.
[56] Herring, Criminal Law, p. 126.
[57] Ashworth, Principles of Criminal Law, p. 117.
[58] Wells, Crim.L.F. 1995, p. 60.

ultimately gave birth to the homonymous directing mind theory used to establish mens rea on part of a company.

2.4.4 Aggregation of Fault

The directing mind theory found its first application in a manslaughter case in the prosecution that followed the Herald of Free Enterprise Capsize.[59] As mentioned earlier, leaving the bow doors open was identified as the immediate reason that caused the ship to sink, highlighting the crew member's responsibility to close these doors. Yet the report revealed that the company failed to maintain sufficient safety standards. The company did not utilize a chain of responsibility to notice the absence of that particular crew member, or that the bow doors were still open, or a technical system which could have indicated such a failure. Thus, fault must lay higher in the company and not only in one individual. The report concluded: "All in management [...] were guilty of fault in that all must be regarded as sharing the responsibility."[60]

This shared responsibility is what ultimately caused the manslaughter trial against P&O European Ferries to collapse. During the evidential hearing the trial judge could not be convinced that the prosecution was able to establish mens rea in one employee senior enough to represent the company.[61] The necessity to identify a senior employee or directing mind with the company for mens rea offences became clear in *Tesco v Nattrass*, a case in which mens rea was held by one individual. But in scenarios in which responsibility and likewise mens rea are shared by a group of individuals, mens rea must still be held in full by one single person in order to be assigned to a company. Therefore, the trial judge ruled that fault cannot be aggregated[62], because the law prohibits this aggregation for convictions of individuals and hence for companies.[63]

---

[59] Ibid, pp. 62.
[60] H.M. Coroner for East Kent ex parte Spooner, 88 Crim. App. at 10.
[61] Wells, Criminal Law Forum 1995, p. 63.
[62] Ibid, p. 64.
[63] Herring, Criminal Law, p. 123.

Despite its unfortunate ending, the P&O prosecution had significant influence on corporate criminality: It abolished the last doubts that a corporation could not be indicted with manslaughter according to English law.[64]

2.4.5 Size matters

The first successful corporate manslaughter prosecution in the history of the UK also revealed another weakness of the Directing Mind Theory. The prosecution followed the death of four children while on a canoe trip.[65] The children neither received proper training nor adequate equipment and the trip was supervised by unqualified staff.[66] One trainer even left the company because he was not satisfied with the safety standards. The Managing Director was sentenced to three years imprisonment and the company was fined £60,000.[67]

The burden of satisfying the identification doctrine was facilitated by the company's flat organisational hierarchy. The company that organised the trip consisted of two directors and only a few employees. Therefore, the mens rea was not splintered across a whole organisational body.[68] The prosecution could easily prove that the company's owner held the mens rea in full instead of having to aggregate fault as in the P & O European Ferries case. Thus, the likelihood of a successful conviction of an indicted company declines non-proportional with its size. While in small companies the "Directing Minds" tend to be virtually identical with the company, in larger firms many functions will be delegated to middle or lower management. [69]

2.4.6 Expanding the Identification Theory

In the case of Meridian Funds v Security Commission[70] that came shortly after the conviction of OII Ltd. the courts were willing to expand the identification

---

[64] R. v. P&O European Ferries (Dover) 1999. Wells, Criminal Law Forum 1995, p. 64.
[65] R. v. OII Ltd.; Keenan, English Law, p. 683.
[66] Slapper, NLJ Practitioner 1994, p. 1735.
[67] Slapper, The Changing Legal Scenery, p. 3.
[68] Keenan, English Law, p. 683.
[69] Dunford / Ridley, ILJ 1997, p.107.
[70] Meridian Global Funds Management Asia Ltd. v. Securities Commission [1995].

doctrine beyond the directing mind. The case concerned a company which was taken to court by the Securities Commission because two of its investment officers bought shares without giving notice as required by law, unknowingly to the board of directors. The courts should be prepared to interpret legislation in order to determine who can be considered a directing mind and will of the company for the purpose of the offence in question.[71] In this case the court indeed decided to impute the officers' minds as the company's will although they normally would not have accounted for a directing mind.[72]

However, this expansion of the identification doctrine is limited. It was considered in the manslaughter prosecution of Great Western Trains which followed the Southall Rail Crash. But the court of appeal rejected the flexibility introduced by Meridian Funds. It was held that this interpretation might create injustice if the acts or minds of all employees can be attributed to a company that is actually blameless.[73]

2.5 Conclusion: The Present Situation

The failed prosecutions for Corporate Manslaughter constitute a breach with the government's desire to provide safe communities. While the first case of a company indicted with manslaughter dates back to the 1920's, real acceptance of corporate criminality within this sphere followed 60 years later. Since then, cases of corporate manslaughter were handled by the common law principles of gross negligence manslaughter. Those principles were designed to punish individual fault and consequently have been proven to be inadequate to punish corporate fault. The weaknesses of the identification and directing mind theories were highlighted by various prosecutions for "corporate" manslaughter.[74]

The current law on corporate manslaughter has been blurred up to a point at which even the director of prosecutions was not sure anymore which cases were

---

[71] Clarkson, Corporate Culpability, p. 6.
[72] Dunford / Ridley, ILJ 1997, p. 106.
[73] Ashworth, Principles of Criminal Law, p. 118.
[74] Almond, Law & Policy, p. 287.

likely to be squashed and which promised a successful conviction.[75] In R v British Steel the company tried to avoid (although unsuccessfully) a conviction under the HSWA after two workers were killed, by bringing forward the identification principle.[76]

The public's concerns are that the current standard of law neglects the unlawful conduct of corporations, which cause the death of persons in exercise of their business activities.[77] These concerns have risen with the number of unsuccessful prosecutions.[78] Instead, more convictions were brought under the category of regulatory law. However, this legislation, such as the HSWA, aims at maintaining safety standards and not punishing wrongdoers.[79] The Law Commission recognized the public's perception in its report on reforming the law on involuntary manslaughter in 1994. The necessity of legal change became clear.

3.0 The Corporate Manslaughter Act 2007

3.1 Introduction

The inappropriateness of gross negligence manslaughter for a corporate defendant was already reflected by the various decisions of the courts before the Law Commission addressed the issue in its report on reforming the Criminal Code in 1994 for the first time.[80] Nonetheless, it took over a decade from the initial proposals of this report to the final bill to be passed by Parliament. This long period of discussion not only stresses the delicacy of the topic, but the debate was additionally prolonged by a General Election that made the government lose its commitment to changing the law.[81]

---

[75] In R v DPP ex parte Timothy Jones [2000] the DPP had to reconsider his decision not to prosecute because he applied a wrong test. Slapper, Corporate Manslaughter, p. 2.
[76] R. v. British Steel [1995]. See, also Dunford / Ridley, ILJ 1997, pp. 104.
[77] Home Office, Corporate Manslaughter Draft Bill, paras. 8-12. See, Almond, Law & Policy, p. 287.
[78] Dunford / Ridley, ILJ 1997, p. 112.
[79] Clarkson, Crim.L.R, pp. 677-678.
[80] Law Commission Consultation Paper No. 135 1994.
[81] Watkins, JotP 2005, p.488.

After a brief overview of the content and arguments of this discussion, this part begins with a summary of the offence's aims and definition. Then it continues with a detailed analysis of the various elements of the offence starting with its expanded sphere of application and ending with the possible penalties. This analysis is fundamental for the subsequent comparison of the former and the new situation, which focuses on their differences and similarities. It shows how the government's proposals have been perceived by the public and other representatives. The part concludes on the effectiveness of the offence with respect to the precedent comparison and determines if the government will be likely to achieve its aims.

3.2 Legal History of the Corporate Manslaughter Act

The Law Commission's consultation paper 135 shortly followed the conviction of OLL Ltd. The report recognized the shortcomings of the legal system to address grossly careless failures of companies that result in death and the public concern over these shortcomings.[82] It further suggested a special regime regarding corporate liability for manslaughter that bases liability not solely on identification with a human being.[83] The responses to the Law Commission's consultation paper were overwhelmingly positive and only a minority completely rejected the idea of corporate responsibility for manslaughter.[84] Following the consultation paper, the Law Commission discussed the possibilities of introducing a new statutory offence in its report on Legislating the Criminal Code: Involuntary Manslaughter of 1996.[85] The report proposed the new offence of corporate killing by gross carelessness.[86] A corporation could be convicted of this offence if an organisation's management failure has led to the death of persons whose health and safety must be ensured by the organisation,

---

[82] Law Commission, Consultation Paper 135, paras. 4.21 - 4.25.
[83] Law Commission, Report 237, para 7.5.
[84] Ibid, para. 7.7.
[85] Law Commission, Report 237, parts 6-8.
[86] Ibid, para. 8.1.

and if the defendant's conduct fell below what could have reasonably been expected.[87]

The government widely accepted the Law Commission's proposals.[88] Dispute arose only around a few facts. While the Law Commission foresaw only incorporated bodies to be caught by the offence, the Government wished to include all unincorporated bodies by replacing the term with undertakings.[89] Another point of disagreement was to what extent individual liability should be included in the offence. The Law Commission rejected any individual liability in a corporate offence, whereas the government was willing to include it.[90]

The draft bill, initially planned to be published in 2003, was finally released in March 2005.[91] The final bill included the Law Commission's initial proposals with a few alterations and was introduced to the House of Commons in July 2006. After one year of debate the Corporate Manslaughter and Corporate Homicide Act 2007 was passed on 26th July 2007.

3.3 The Government's Targets

The Corporate Manslaughter Act seeks to tackle the key difficulty to a successful corporate manslaughter prosecution according to common law: the need to prove that a directing mind, an embodiment of the company, is itself guilty of manslaughter.[92] Corporations and other organisations shall be held liable properly for their actions with fatal consequences.[93] Yet, the government is interested in keeping a careful balance between the society's need to a criminal prosecution in such incidents and laws that restrict business activity or create a "risk averse" culture.[94] The offence shall complement but not replace existing

---

[87] Ibid, para. 8.3.5.
[88] Peck / Brevitt, Research Paper 06/46, p. 11.
[89] Home Office, Involuntary Manslaughter Government's Proposals, para.3.2.1 - 3.2.8.
[90] Ibid, para. 3.4.5 – 3.4.9.
[91] Peck / Brevitt, Research Paper 06/46, p. 13-14.
[92] Home Office, Corporate Manslaughter Draft Bill, p.4.
[93] Watkins, JotP 2005, p. 490.
[94] Home Office, Corporate Manslaughter Draft Bill, p. 6, para. 3.

health and safety regulations.[95] Thus, a prosecution for corporate manslaughter must be reserved for the worst cases. Finally, the Act aims at restoring the public faith that the government is able to handle corporate crime[96], by providing a clear and effective offence, and more importantly, within the sphere of criminal, not civil law.

3.4 The Offence in Brief

The Corporate Manslaughter Act creates the new offence of Corporate Manslaughter in England.[97] The offence replaces the application of manslaughter by gross negligence within the corporate sphere.[98]

An organisation will be liable under this provision if it owes a duty of care to another person and if the ways the organisation manages or organises its activities constitute a gross breach of that duty and caused the other person's death.[99] An organisation found guilty of corporate manslaughter may be fined and ordered to remedy its failures under this act.[100] While this short definition appears to be remotely identical to the former gross negligence offence, it contains various elements of different aspects.

3.5 Scope of the Offence

The above-mentioned elements deserve further attention to understand their meaning for the corporate manslaughter offence.

---

[95] Ibid, p. 4.
[96] Home Office, Involuntary Manslaughter Government's Proposals, p.13, para. 3.1.5
[97] Home Office, Corporate Manslaughter Act Explanatory Notes, p. 1, para. 3.
[98] Ibid.
[99] Corporate Manslaughter and Corporate Homicide Act 2007, cl. 1(1).
[100] Ibid, cl. 1(6).

3.5.1 Application

Despite the Law Commission's initial idea to include only incorporated bodies in the offence and the draft bill did not provide for unincorporated bodies to be caught by the offence[101], the offence offers a rather broad scope of application in its final version. Now, it addresses corporations and various public institutions including the police force.[102] Institutions under this offence that formerly could not be prosecuted, no longer enjoy crown immunity.[103] But liability of the public institutions caught by the offence is limited as described later. The Corporate Manslaughter Act also applies to unincorporated bodies like business partnerships and trade unions, with the requirement of those organisations being an employer. Thus, the application of the offence is closer to the government's idea to include all undertakings and not solely incorporated bodies. [104]

3.5.2 Relevant Duty of Care

The starting points of this offence are the obligations owed by the employer (the organisation) to a number of addressees. To be liable under the corporate manslaughter act an organisation must have owed a relevant duty of care to the deceased.[105] This concerns duties like the employer's obligation under the Health and Safety at Work Act to provide a safe workplace. Most of these duties are of civil law nature.[106] The relevance of these duties with respect to public institutions is further defined in the act.[107] Although these institutions no longer enjoy crown immunity, a prosecution will not be possible if the duty concerns execution of an exclusively public function.[108] It is ultimately a question of law

---

[101] Home Office, Corporate Manslaughter Draft Bill, p. 14, paras. 34-35.
[102] Corporate Manslaughter and Corporate Homicide Act 2007, cl. 1(2).
[103] Ibid, cl. 11(1).
[104] Home Office, Corporate Manslaughter Act Explanatory Notes, pp. 3, para. 16.
[105] Corporate Manslaughter and Corporate Homicide Act 2007, cl. 1(1b).
[106] Peck / Brevitt, Research Paper 06/46, p. 21.
[107] Corporate Manslaughter and Corporate Homicide Act 2007, cl. 2-7.
[108] The purpose is of this limitation is to prevent the prosecution of public bodies for activities that are supposed to benefit the Community. Home Office, Corporate Manslaughter Act Explanatory Notes, p. 6, paras. 23-26. Also, Watkins, JotP 2005, p. 490.

whether the organisation owes a duty of care to the other person and, thus, the judge must answer that question.[109]

Once it has been established that the organisation owed a duty of care to the deceased, it must be shown that it was in breach of that duty.[110] The breach of duty must have been gross. It is ultimately up to the jury to decide if the alleged breach was gross, but the prosecution needs to provide evidence.[111] In general, the jury may consider any matters relevant to the issues, but should have specific regard to health and safety guidance and the company's internal policies and systems.

Thus, after the judge has put this question to jury, it will have to balance the harm caused by the misconduct and the precautions taken in order to avoid the harm. This balancing process requires intense knowledge of industry standards, making the reference to health safety guidance essential. [112]

3.5.3 Gross Breach

The alleged breach of a duty will be considered gross if the organisation's conduct that led to the breach fell far below what can be reasonably expected of the organisation in the circumstances.[113] This saves manslaughter prosecutions to incidents in which failing on part of the organisation have been exceptionally grave and corporate manslaughter prosecutions will be reserved only for the worst cases of management failure.[114] This appears to contradict the intention to facilitate corporate manslaughter prosecutions but expresses the government's desire to avoid wholesale prosecutions. [115]

---

[109] Home Office, Corporate Manslaughter Draft Bill, p. 39, para. 27.
[110] Corporate Manslaughter and Corporate Homicide Act 2007, cl. 1 (1b).
[111] Ibid, cl. 8 (1-2). Watkins, JotP 2005, p. 491.
[112] Dunford / Ridley, ILJ 1997, p. 109.
[113] The Corporate Manslaughter and Corporate Homicide Act 2007, cl. 1 (4b).
[114] Watkins, JotP 2005, p. 490.
[115] Ibid.

3.5.4 New Identification

The alleged gross breach of a duty of care must have been caused by the way the organisation manages its activities. This is also referred to as a management failure. The Law Commission originally intended to remove the border of identification from a corporate manslaughter prosecution.[116] Culpability would have been only contingent upon a management failure without having to identify an individual.[117] The purpose is to put the focus on general methods and practices used by organisation rather than day to day activities by single employees.[118] Yet, in the corporate manslaughter offence it remains contingent upon the substantial involvement of a senior manager in the failure.[119] Therefore, the offence foresees a change from individual to corporate culpability as reference is made to management failure but retains the controlling mind requirement (although in a mitigated form).[120] Identification was not removed, but repackaged.

The Prosecution is further limited by another requirement: The Director of Prosecution's consent to lay charges against an organisation. Otherwise, any citizen would be able to stipulate a proceeding against an organisation. Although this seems to raise the bar to a prosecution higher, it is necessary to protect the organisations, especially the ones that formerly enjoyed crown immunity, from being prosecuted for virtually anything.[121]

3.5.5 No Individual Liability

The Law Commission initially foresaw that no individual should be liable under an exclusively corporate offence. Individual liability should only arise when the persons themselves are guilty of manslaughter.[122] The government opposed that position and questioned the deterrent of the offence without punitive

---

[116] Law Commission, Report 237, para. 7.5.
[117] Ibid, pp. 110-122, paras. 8.36-8.39.
[118] Dunford / Ridley, ILJ 1997, p. 110.
[119] Peck / Brevitt, Research Paper 06/46, p. 36.
[120] Watkins, JotP 2005, p. 490.
[121] Ibid.
[122] Law Commission, Report 237, pp. 118, paras. 8.56-8.58.

sanctions against individuals. According to the government's proposals an individual could have even faced imprisonment if his behaviour contributed to corporate manslaughter.[123] But the government dropped the idea of individual liability in a corporate offence after it received quite diversified opinions on its suggestions.[124] The Corporate Manslaughter Act thus does not provide for such secondary liability.[125] However, the HSWA provides for accessory liability of individuals.[126]

3.5.6 Penalties

An organisation liable under this offence is subject to indictment of an unlimited fine.[127] In addition, the court may order the convicted organisation to remedy any matters or deficiencies that may have been relevant to the breach of duty and might have caused the death.[128] Furthermore, the court may order the organisation to publicise the details of its conviction and fine as well as the remedial order's terms.[129] Should the organisation fail to comply with either the remedial order or the publicity order, it will be liable to indictment of another fine.[130]

Although a mere monetary penalty was originally considered an adequate remedy, the Law Commission's proposals of 1996 already foresaw a remedial order as an additional remedy.[131] Initially, the offence also provided for responsible individuals to be subject to disqualification, but since the final version precludes individual liability this provision was dropped.[132] Furthermore, some concerns remained upon the fining of public bodies. This "recycling" of public money allegedly serves no practical purpose but merely signals culpability.[133]

---

[123] Home Office, Involuntary Manslaughter Government's Proposals, pp. 19, paras. 3.4.7-3.4.13.
[124] Home Office, Corporate Manslaughter Draft Bill, p. 17, para. 47.
[125] Corporate Manslaughter and Corporate Homicide Act 2007, cl. 18.
[126] HSWA cl. 37 (1).
[127] Corporate Manslaughter and Corporate Homicide Act 2007, cl. 1 (6).
[128] Ibid, cl. 9.
[129] Ibid, cl. 10.
[130] Ibid, cl. 9 (5) and cl. 10 (4).
[131] Dunford / Ridley, ILJ 1997, p. 111. Law Commission, Report 237, pp. 123, paras. 8.72-8.76.
[132] Watkins, JotP 2005, p. 491.
[133] Peck / Brevitt, Research Paper 06/46, p. 40.

3.6 Changes from Gross Negligence to Corporate Manslaughter

In order to compare the new and the former provisions for corporate manslaughter, it is necessary to keep in mind the old test for gross negligence manslaughter established in Adomako and Attorney's General Reference No. 2 of 1999.[134] This test was considered to neglect the reality of corporate decision-making and therefore inappropriate for corporate defendants. The Government and the Law Commission recognized those considerations and new test for management-failure (instead of identification).

The starting point of the new offence is still a duty of care. The duty of care in gross negligence manslaughter originated from the tort of negligence. In corporate manslaughter the same duties under the law of negligence are used. The new notion of relevance of a duty of care simply emphasizes that not all duties of care can be considered. However, this notion is not without difficulties as it explicitly refers to the law of negligence which limits the concept of a duty of care.[135]

For a company to be in breach of that duty, it was formerly a necessity to establish the actus reus and mens rea against an individual who is an embodiment of the organisation. This method of identification was useful as companies (and other legal entities) cannot act on their own, but only through their agents and servants. The application of the offence has been extended widely, most thankfully to the abolishment of crown immunity. Still, those organisations cannot act by themselves and, hence, identification remained a contingency in the form of substantial involvement of a senior manager.[136] Furthermore, a manager will only be deemed senior for the purpose of this offence, if he plays a significant role about how the whole or substantial parts of the "company" are managed (not parts of the company in his own sphere of

---

[134] See above chapter 3.0.
[135] Clarkson, CLR 2005, p. 683.
[136] It is questionable whether a management failure model is possible without any reference to individuals. Wells, Crim.L.R., p. 552.

responsibility). It is hard to envisage how any person other than a director can have such a role.[137]

A breach of duty according to *Adomako* is gross if the defendant could reasonably foresee a risk and if his or her conduct fell far below a reasonable standard. The government's proposals originally provided a clause that senior managers must have foreseen or ought to have foreseen a risk. This provision did not persevere in the Corporate Manslaughter Act. In its final version, the standard of grossness is solely determined by the question if the conduct fell far below what could have been reasonably expected. This focus is in line with the Court of Appeal's decision in Attorney General's Reference (No.2 of 1999), which stated that the jury may convict a defendant although he had not foreseen that the victim would be killed.[138] Hence, the new Corporate Manslaughter Offence offers a standard of grossness similar to the old test for manslaughter by gross negligence.[139]

The penalties for corporate manslaughter come in the form of a monetary fine and remedial and publicity orders. Apart from the publicity order, those penalties are virtually identical with the penalties that can be imposed under the HSWA.[140] A monetary fine was also the primary penalty imposed on corporations guilty of gross negligence manslaughter as a legal person cannot be imprisoned.[141] Yet, the majority of corporations were prosecuted for violating the HSWA and not the offence of manslaughter, because of the above-shown legal obstacles. Therefore, more penalties were imposed on corporations under the provisions of the HSWA. There is little to no change in the sphere of penalties.[142]

---

[137] Watkins, JotP 2005, p. 491. Also, Clarkson, CLR 2005, p. 683.
[138] Herring, Criminal Law, p. 125.
[139] Almond, Law & Policy 2007, p. 288.
[140] Watkins, JotP, p. 169. Also, HSWA s. 42 (1).
[141] Ashworth,
[142] Clarkson and Watkins criticize that the offence lacks any individual liability. Clarkson, Crim.L.R. 2005, p. 689. Watkins, JotP 2005, p. 169.

3.7 Conclusion: Reactions to the Changes

The Corporate Manslaughter Bill was recently given royal assent and waits to be enacted in 2008. Therefore, the real implications of the new offence remain to be seen once the first organisations have been charged with corporate manslaughter. Yet several factors indicate its limited success in the future.

In fact, only little change has been achieved. The pure "management-failure"-approach without the senior manager requirement as envisaged by the Law Commission did not make it into the final act. The penalties under the Corporate Manslaughter Act are quasi the same as under the HSWA. The fact that those fines were included in a corporate offence within the boundaries of the criminal law serves a symbolic purpose to reflect the seriousness of manslaughter.[143] The same must apply to the impact a publicity order may have on the public's perception of a company. However, as the number of prosecutions is unlikely to increase and many corporations might still "get away with murder" it is questionable if the offence will satisfy this symbolic purpose.[144]

Shortly after the Law Commission published its report No. 237 legal authors appreciated the removal of the identification requirement and anticipated an increase of successful prosecutions.[145] Yet, some scepticism remained on the unusually high degree of jury involvement in the judgement.[146] After it became apparent that the government intended to keep the identification doctrine as a part of the offence, authors reacted very critically and questioned the success of the law reform.[147] "[...] This Bill [...] will achieve neither an increase in safety nor provide the public with the confidence in the criminal justice system."[148] The test originally intended for management failure would have placed the focus on

---

[143] Almond, Law & Policy 2007, p. 288.
[144] Ibid, p. 305.
[145] Dunford / Ridley, ILJ 1997, p. 112.
[146] Ibid,
[147] Clarkson, Almond, and Watkins reject the senior manager test and prefer the Law Commission's initial proposals. Watkins, JotP 2005, p. 492; Clarkson, CLR 2005, p. 689; Almond, Law & Policy, p. 288.
[148] Watkins, JotP 2005, p. 492.

corporate decisions and activities but the senior manager requirement seems to have lost sight of that focus.[149]

While many commentators criticized the statute, it has reached its goals from a government's perspective. The government created a new criminal offence applicable to organisations that abolishes the need to find a culpable directing mind in order to convict an organisation but preserves the identification principle. The senior management requirement will prevent a drastic increase of prosecutions, a fact that has been widely criticized. But as the government never intended to provide for "wholesale prosecutions" in the act anyway, this is in line with its targeted limitations. The business leaders agree with the government's sensible approach to corporate liability.[150]

4.0 The Act in Comparison with German Law

4.1 Introduction

It would be wrong to think that incidents like the ones mentioned in the beginning are unique to the UK. As corporations exist globally the outcome of their actions, whether positive or negative, must occur likewise in other countries, too. But as mentioned in the beginning, not every country treats corporations the same. One of the latest cases of manslaughter by gross negligence in Germany is the ICE rail crash near Eschede.

In 1998 the ICE train named "Wilhem Conrad Röntgen" crashed after one wheel broke off an axle and was forced into the train's floor. Another part of the wheel hit a switch causing the third wagon to derail. The train struck the bridge it was about to pass under, which collapsed and crushed several wagons. More than 100 persons died in that rail crash. The main cause of the accident was the newly developed type of wheel the Deutsche Bahn AG chose to operate on its

---

[149] Clarkson, Crim.L.R. 2005, p. 684.
[150] "Business welcome corporate killing bill" – Financial Times 23 July 2006.

ICE trains. The new wheels were available at a lower price, but the Deutsche Bahn knew that they had not been sufficiently tested yet.

This case of manslaughter offers a pattern of fault similar to the ones from the UK presented in the beginning.[151] Although individual fault has contributed to the ultimate cause, assuming a corporate guilt appears to be more adequate. Nonetheless, bringing criminal charges against the Deutsche Bahn AG could not even be considered. Although the company was fined for each deceased, the criminal prosecution focused on individuals. This indicates a substantial difference to the British solution.

This part focuses first on identifying this difference by comparing the offence of corporate manslaughter to the German equivalent Fahrlässige Tötung. Then it investigates other remedies according to German law, concentrating on the Ordnungswidrigkeitenrecht. Subsequently it analyzes the differences and similarities of the German and the British solutions by comparing both concepts. Finally this part concludes on the necessity of a corporate manslaughter offence at German law.

4.2 Manslaughter at German Law

4.2.1 Fahrlässige Tötung[152]

The most appropriate corresponding criminal offence to gross negligence manslaughter at German Law would be Fahrlässige Tötung. As in gross negligence manslaughter, the criminal act can either be by conduct or by an omission of a duty[153], but in any case must be fahrlässig[154] (below what could have been expected of the offender in the given circumstances[155]). In addition,

---

[151] Another incident was recently the focus of the media's attention. During the pregnant women were given a potentially harmful medication produced by the company Grünthal. This medication caused severe mutilations to their infants. Approximately half of the inflicted people have died by today. "Verursacher in der Pflicht" – Berliner Morgenpost 11th November 2007.
[152] §222 StGB
[153] Schönke / Schröder / Eser, StGB, 27th ed., §222, para. 2a
[154] §15 StGB
[155] Schönke / Schröder / Cramer / Sternberg-Lieben, StGB, 27th ed., §15, para. 116

if the alleged cause of death was Pflichtwidriges Unterlassen (breach of a duty by ommission), this must have also been the proximate cause of death[156].

4.2.2 Elements of a Criminal Offence: Comparison

The British and the German legal frameworks have a similar concept of a criminal offence. Both assume that an unlawful act must consist of *objektive Tatbestände* (actus reus) and *subjektive Tatbestände* (mens rea)[157]. The British jurisdiction struggled to attribute mens rea to legal persons, but gradually developed several theories to overcome this problem. The British system has adopted the theory that the subjektive Tatbestände may relate to failures which go beyond individual responsibility and, thus, express a corporate fault. This acceptance has led to a real criminal liability for corporations.[158] As the concepts of a criminal offence are alike, one might be tempted to believe that juristic persons are likewise accepted as criminal offenders. Yet, at German law a juristic person cannot be guilty of a criminal offence.

4.2.3 No Corporate Liability at the Penal Code

A juristic person, whether company or non-profit organisation, cannot commit a Straftat at German law.[159] Instead, only the natural individuals will be criminally liable for their actions at work.[160] In addition, directors and senior managers may have a stronger liability as they also exercise decisive, controlling, and supervisory powers.

Contrary to the well established individual liability, legal persons cannot be the target of criminal liability mainly for three reasons. They cannot act themselves, but only through their agents.[161] A mere attribution of their agents' actions is insufficient for a Straftat.[162] Further, they lack the culpability necessary to

---

[156] Ibid, §13, para. 80.
[157] Ackermann, Die juristische Person, p. 77.
[158] Haeusermann, Der Verband als Straftäter, pp. 60.
[159] Eidam, Unternehmen und Strafe, p. 155.
[160] Ibid.
[161] Eidam, Straftäter Unternehmen, p. 91.
[162] Freier, Kritik der Verbandsstrafe, p. 88.

commit a Straftat.[163] Lastly, corporations lack the ability to realize the fault of their actions, and their punishment would fail to achieve the ultimate goal of a Kriminalstrafe; to atone for the crime.[164]

Therefore, the German penal code is only concerned with individual fault and offers a variety of means to redeem the latter. Where criminal fault as part of the individual's employment is concerned, liability rests with each employee within the sphere of his employment.[165] Going further, §14 StGB[166] expresses a provision which punishes the individual who acts for a corporation although the offence addresses the latter. The intention is to avoid legal loopholes by concentrating solely on individual liability even though some offences address legal persons. [167]

The only provision in the penal code concerned with corporations is §73 StGB, "Wirkung des Verfalls". Under this provision, a court may order the Verfall of any profits or objects if they were unlawfully obtained by an individual. The Verfall may be ordered against legal persons instead if the actual offender has acted for the latter. However, §73 StGB is not concerned with corporate liability and does not constitute a form of corporate punishment.[168]

4.3 Remedies at German Law

Although the German law system offers no remedy from a real criminal law point of view, a legal person can be punished under the Ordnungswidrigkeitengesetz (OWiG). However, it is important to note that this must not be confused with a criminal offence. Contrary to the latter, a penalty according to the OWiG seeks to punish misconduct without criminal content[169].

---

[163] Eidam, Straftäter Unternehmen, p. 92
[164] Ibid, p. 93.
[165] Eidam, Unternehmen und Strafe, p. 155.
[166] Similar, §9 OWiG.
[167] Eidam, Unternehmen und Strafe, pp. 182.
[168] Ehrhardt, Unternehmensdelinquenz, pp. 39.
[169] Eidam, Unternehmen und Strafe, p. 110.

Its purpose is rather to maintain law and order and not to revenge a crime.[170] Therefore, the Ordnungswidrigkeitenrecht is remotely similar to the regulatory offences at British Law.[171]

4.3.1 „Geldbuße gegen Juristische Personen"[172]

Under §30 OWiG a legal person can be fined if its representatives have been found guilty of a (criminal) offence.[173] Thus, the German law acknowledges corporate liability, but only within the boundaries of its Ordnungswidrigkeitenrecht.[174]

A legal person, nicht rechtsfähige Vereine, and rechtsfähige Personen-gesellschaften may be fined under this provision. This includes incorporated organisations, non-profit organisations and public institutions.[175] To be liable under this provision it is required that a legal representative must have breached a duty that concerns the legal person or committed an offence from which the legal person profited.[176] Initially only the legal agents were considered as representatives. With the amendments made to this provision, the term was extended to include Prokuristen, Handlungsbevollmächtige and other Leitungs- or Führungspersonen. Now the persons that may trigger corporate liability start from a senior manager level expanding upwards.[177] Hence this provision offers a scope of application similar to the Corporate Manslaughter Act. In any case, the offender must have a role as a representative of the legal person that is sufficient enough to have Vertretungsbezug.[178] Here, the focus lies on the functions of the representative and his conduct.[179] An act of an individual will have Vertretungsbezug if his conduct is part of the represented person's goals and policies.[180]

---

[170] Ibid.
[171] Haeusermann, Der Verband als Straftäter, p. 59.
[172] §30 OWiG.
[173] Senge / Rogall, OWiG, 3rd ed., §30, p. 487, para. 1.
[174] Ibid. However, German law knows corporate *vicarious* liability for corporations at §31 BGB.
[175] Ibid, para. 30.
[176] §30 (1) para. 5 OWiG.
[177] Bahnmüller, Strafrechtliche Unternehmensverantwortlichkeit, p. 49.
[178] Müller, Die Stellung der juristischen Person im OWiG, p. 76.
[179] Senge / Rogall, OWiG, 3rd ed., §30, p. 512, para. 90.
[180] Ibid, para. 91.

4.3.2 Bezugstat

A juristic person under §30 OWiG will be liable if one of its legal representatives has been found guilty of a (criminal) offence.[181] Thus, this provision always connects to another person committing a Straftat or Ordnungswidrigkeit, the offence that connects to §30 OWiG is called Bezugstat.[182] The juristic person must have either profited from the Bezugstat or be in breach of a duty resulting from the misconduct. If the liability results from a breach of a duty, this duty must be betriebsbezogen.[183] This includes duties that concern the owner of a company or the company as such. In general, Allgemeindelikte are not within the scope of this definition, unless they involve breach of a betriebsbezogene Pflicht.[184] However, it is not essential if the Bezugstat was committed by conduct or omission, only the breach of the duty is relevant to the Bezugstat. Thus, fahrlässige Tötung can be a Bezugstat of §30 OWiG if a breach of duty is a result of the Bezugstat and if that duty was addressed to the corporation.[185]

4.3.3 Geldbuße

A juristic person found guilty under §30 can be sanctioned with a fine.[186] Usually, the individual and the corporation will be sanctioned in a combined process (Kumulative Verbandsgeldbuße).[187] However, it is also possible to sanction the corporation even if the charges against any individual were dropped or the decision was made not to prosecute (Isolierte Verbandsgeldbuße)[188]. Finally, it is also possible to fine the corporation if the actual offender cannot be identified, but it can be proven that the Bezugstat was committed by a person that meets the necessary qualifications (Anonyme Verbandsgeldbuße)[189]. Furthermore, should the corporation not be sanctioned by a monetary fine, it can be ordered that any profits that are a result of the

---

[181] §30 (1) OWiG.
[182] Müller, Die Stellung der juristischen Person im OWiG, p. 72.
[183] Senge / Rogall, OwiG, 3rd ed., §30, p. 508, para. 72.
[184] Ibid.
[185] Schroth, Unternehmen als Normadressaten, p. 46.
[186] §30 (1) para. 5.
[187] Senge / Rogall, OwiG, 3rd ed., §30, p. 514, para. 100.
[188] Ibid, para. 101.
[189] Ibid, para. 102.

misconduct will be withdrawn from the corporation.[190] The maximum fines that can be imposed under §30 OWiG are €500,000 if the Bezugstat was a crime of negligence and €100,000 if it was a voluntary crime.[191]

4.3.4 Similarities of Corporate Manslaughter and §30 OWiG

The conceptual difference of the OWiG and the StGB notwithstanding, the Vebandsbuße offers a possibility to sanction juristic persons for the fault of their representatives.[192] The guilt and the misconduct of the employees will be imputed to the company as its own failure, thus this provision is considered a "Zurechnungsnorm".[193]

While it is rather easy to find a duty of care of relevance to the corporation that has been breached, as both systems offer a quite broad scope of mandatory duties at law, problems might occur to find a culpable individual. The British and the German concepts require identification of an individual culpable of the offence of manslaughter before the company itself can be indicted[194]. While the British system converted this process into the criminal offence of corporate manslaughter and consequently tried to facilitate the process of identification (although questionable) by adopting the theory of management failure, the German system still relies on imputing the sole culpability of an individual to the company. This concept has hindered the successful prosecution of corporations in the UK and in Germany.[195]

4.4 Regulatory or Criminal Offence?

The British and the German legal code distinguish criminal and regulatory offences. The meaning of a penalty imposed under a regulatory offence like HSWA was considered inadequate to punish the criminal wrongdoing of

---

[190] Senge / Rogall, OwiG, 3rd ed., §30, p. 515, para. 106. Similar, §73 StGB.
[191] §30 (2) paras. 1-2 OWiG.
[192] Eidam, Unternehmen und Strafe, p. 204.
[193] Tiedemann, NJW 1988, p. 1172.
[194] Bahnmüller, Strafrechtliche Unternehmensverantwortlichkeit, S. 47
[195] Ibid.

corporations in the UK[196], although the sanctions under the HSWA and corporate manslaughter offence are virtually the same. However, a conviction under the HSWA stipulates less seriousness to the crime of manslaughter and violates the principle of "fair labelling".[197] This leads to the question whether an Ordnungswidrigkeit can be a sufficient replacement to a criminal offence according to German law. To consider this question it is necessary to point out the differences of the OWiG and the StGB.

4.4.1 Differences of OWiG and StGB

From a mere formal point of view the OWiG can be distinguished from the StGB by the subsequent penalty. While a violation of an offence under the OWiG will result in a Geldbuße, the StGB foresees a Kriminalstrafe.[198] However, those penalties also differ materially.

A Kriminalstrafe is a public judgement on the shameful, unlawful, and culpable misconduct of the offender.[199] The offender is invited to atone for his crime.[200] Furthermore it deters the occurrence of any further delinquent acts of the offender.[201] A Geldbuße under the OWiG can have a similar if not the same meaning.[202]

4.4.2 Prevention

Although the Verbandsbuße is generally considered merely a reminder of a person's duties, it can have also a repressive function as the German word "Buße" already indicates. The Geldbuße connects to a culpable, unlawful act.[203]

---

[196] Clarkson, Crim.L.R. 2005, p.688.
[197] Ibid, p. 687. Clarkson also points out that the title manslaughter already violates this principle as it is a crime of violence and this term wrongly reflects such incidents. He prefers the more neutral notion of "Corporate Killing".
[198] Bahnmüller, Strafrechtliche Unternehmensverantwortlichkeit, p.72.
[199] Jescheck, Lehrbuch des Strafrechts AT, p. 67.
[200] Ehrhardt, Unternehmensdelinquenz, p. 72.
[201] Jescheck, Lehrbuch des Strafrechts AT, p. 68.
[202] Ehrhardt, Unternehmensdelinquenz, p. 74.
[203] Ibid, p. 71.

Therefore, this penalty attempts to prevent future violations from occurring. The Geldbuße and Geldstrafe do not differ regarding prevention.[204]

4.4.3 Condemnation

The main difference of an Ordnungswidrigkeit and a Kriminalstrafe lies in the „sozial-ethisches Unwerturteil". A Kriminalstrafe allegedly does not condemn the immoral misconduct of the offender. However, this is not necessarily true. Such a condemnation always depends on the public perception of a particular crime.[205] In light of this, the public rather looks to the level of the fine than its legal origin, although the reverse situation is often simply presumed.[206] Thus the Verbandsgeldbuße can have a "sozial-ethisches Unwerturteil", as long as the amount a corporation is fined is high enough to satisfy society's perception of justice. [207]

4.4.4 Atonement

Atonement is a process during which the convicted offender realizes and acknowledges the necessity of his punishment.[208] The society shall accept this moral achievement and reconcile with the offender.[209] This supposedly remedies the distorted relation between the individual and the society.[210] However, the state can only invite the offender to atone for his crime, and not force it by punishment.

The Ordnungswidrigkeit is often regarded as a social-ethical neutral, as it only constitutes disobedience with the law.[211] However, every Ordnungswidrigkeit is also a violation of law and order, and thus offers a possibility for atonement.[212]

---

[204] Bahnmüller, Strafrechtliche Unternehmensverantwortlichkeit, p. 79.
[205] Ibid, pp. 80.
[206] Ibid.
[207] Ibid.
[208] Ehrhardt, Unternehmensdelinquenz, p. 72.
[209]Ibid.
[210] Ibid.
[211] Ibid.
[212] Ibid, p. 73.

Furthermore, since the social-ethical neutrality predominantly depends on the level of the fine, this statement is questionable.

From the points discussed it can be argued that the similarity of a Geldbuße and a Geldstrafe strongly depends on the level of the fine imposed.[213] The maximum fines that can be imposed under the OWiG in comparison with those under the StGB can be sufficient to account for the criminal character of an offence.[214] In light of this the Ordnungswidrigkeit and the Kriminalstrafe are remotely identical in their meaning as a legal penalty to corporations.[215]

4.5 Conclusion: The German Solution

The German legal code offers no remedy against corporate fault in its penal code. The reasons for this rejection are almost identical to the ones initially brought forward in the UK. However, it does recognize corporate liability at the BGB and, more importantly, it offers the possibility of sanctioning a corporation for the fault of its representatives at the Ordnungswidrigkeitenrecht which is similar to the British regulatory offences. The concept of the Verbandsgeldbuße works by attributing the failure of legal representatives to the corporation. It always connects to a Straftat or Ordnungswidrigkeit. A Fahrlässige Tötung can be a Bezugstat of §30 OWiG if it involves a breach of a duty which is addressed to the corporation. Crimes of negligence will be punished by a monetary fine in the amount of €500,000.

Yet, the Ordnungswidrigkeitenrecht and Strafrecht differ in purpose and design; hence the Verbandssanktionierung must not be confused with a Kriminalstrafe. In spite of this, those differences are arguably negligible.[216] As a result, German

---

[213] Bahnmüller, Strafrechtliche Unternehmensverantwortlichkeit, p. 81.
[214] Ibid, p. 84.
[215] Ibid, p. 93. However, differences remain regarding the juristic process. Ehrhardt, Unternehmensdelinquenz, p. 73.
[216] Möllering, in Hettinger (Publ.), Strafrechtswissenschaft und Strafrechtspolitik, p. 72.

law knows a corporate offence that barely lacks any essential ingredients of a Kriminalstrafe.[217]

5.0 Conclusion

The British courts developed two doctrines to establish a criminal liability for corporations in addition to their civil law duties. The first doctrine, vicarious liability, was considered too broad to be applied in criminal offences. The identification doctrine imputes the culpability of a legal agent to the corporation in order to establish a corporate culpability. This doctrine showed a lot of difficulties in its application. Thus, the British government decided to introduce the new model of management failure in the Corporate Manslaughter and Corporate Homicide Act 2007. By referring to the way in which the activities of the corporation are managed and organized it tried to facilitate the process of identification.

The question of whether or not the German legal system is in need of the provisions and benefits of a Corporate Manslaughter Act needs to be split in two categories. First, does it lack an offence of manslaughter by gross negligence applicable to corporations? And second, does it lack a criminal corporate offence like the British Corporate Manslaughter Act?

The answer to the first question has to be no. The Geldbuße gegen juristische Personen offers a mean of sanctioning corporations for their delinquency by imputing the fault of their legal representatives like the original British identification doctrine. Then again, the British system has moved forward to a management-failure approach that attempts to reflect the reality of corporate decision-making. But since the identification principle remained contingent to the new offence, little to no change has been achieved and the old problems are

---

[217] Bahnmüller, p. 96.

likely to endure.[218] Thus, both systems have similar ways of punishing corporate fault[219], with the main difference that the German solution is reserved to the Ordnungswidrigkeitenrecht whereas the British System offers a criminal offence in addition to the regulatory offence.

Apart from the legal difficulties of a criminal prosecution, the main criticism to the shortcomings of the British Law was that those incidents were handled by the regulatory law. The regulatory offences are believed to be inadequate to recognize the seriousness of manslaughter. This is not necessarily true for German law. Although German law utilizes a similar separation of serious and less serious offences, an Ordnungswidrigkeit and a Kriminalstrafe are quasi alike with respect to corporate defendants.[220] The purpose and design of the German penal code does not foresee punishment of corporations, in fact it opposes corporate liability. In spite of this, German law does recognize corporate liability according to the BGB and the OWiG.

While it can be questioned why the courts are reluctant to expand this liability into the penal code when the Verbandsgeldbuße at the OWiG is already close to a Kriminalstrafe, this also means that the German legal system is not in serious need of a (criminal) corporate manslaughter offence and[221], therefore, not in need of a Corporate Manslaughter and Corporate Homicide Act 2007.[222]

---

[218] Almond, Law & Policy 2007, p. 288.
[219] Haeusermann, Der Verband als Straftäter, p. 69.
[220] Bahnmüller, Strafrechtliche Unternehmensverantwortlichkeit, p. 93.
[221] Ibid, p. 93 and p. 95.
[222] This does not attempt to answer the question if corporate punishment is viable in general.

Bibliography

Ackermann, Bruni — "Die Strafbarkeit juristischer Personen im deutschen Recht und in ausländischen Rechtsordnungen",
1984,
Peter Lang Frankfurt am Main,
Cited: Die juristische Person.

Almond, Paul — "Regulation Crisis: Evaluating the Potential Legitimizing Effects of Corporate Manslaughter Cases",
2007, in Law & Policy, Vol. 29, No. 3, pp. 285-310.

Ashworth, Andrew — "Principles of Criminal Law",
2006, 5th Edition,
Oxford University Press.

Bahnmüller, Marc — "Strafrechtliche Unternehmensverantwortlichkeit im europäischen Gemeinschafts- und Unionsrecht",
2003,
Peter Lang Frankfurt am Main,
Cited: Strafrechtliche Unternehmensverantwortlichkeit.

Clarkson, C. M. V. — "Corporate Culpability"
1998, in Web Journal of Current Legal Issues,
Blackstone Press Ltd.,
See electronic attachment.

Clarkson, C. M. V. — "Corporate Manslaughter: Yet More Government Proposals"
2005, in Crim.L.R., pp. 677-689.

Dunford / Ridley
Luise & Ann — "Corporate Killing – Legislating for Unlawful Death",
1997, in ILJ, Vol. 26, No. 2. pp, 99-113.

Ehrhardt, Anne — "Unternehmensdelinquenz und Unternehmensstrafe",
1994,
Duncker & Humblot Berlin,
Cited: Unternehmensdelinquenz.

Eidam, Gerd — "Straftäter Unternehmen",
1997,
C. H. Beck München.

Eidam, Gerd — "Unternehmen und Strafe",
1993, 2nd Ed.,
Carl Heymmanns Verlag Köln.

Eisenberg, Melvin — "Corporations and other Business Organisations"
2000, 8th Ed.,
Foundation Press.

Freier, Friedrich von — "Kritik der Verbandsstrafe",
1998,
Duncker & Humblot Berlin.

Haeusermann, Axel	"Der Verband als Straftäter und Strafprozeßobjekt", 2003, Max-Planck-Institut Freiburg, Cited: Der Verband als Straftäter.
Herring, Jonathan	"Criminal Law", 2007, 5th Ed., Palgrave Macmillan Law Masters Oxford.
Home Office	"Reforming the Law on Involuntary Manslaughter: The Government's Proposals" 2000, London: Crown. Cited: Involuntary Manslaughter: Government's Proposals See electronic attachment.
Home Office	"Corporate Manslaughter: The Government's Draft Bill for Reform" 2005, London: The Stationery Office, Cited: Corporate Manslaughter Draft Bill. See electronic attachment.
Home Office	"Corporate Manslaughter and Corporate Homice Act 2007: Explanatory Notes", 2007, London: The Stationery Office, Cited: Corporate Manslaughter Act Explanatory Notes. See electronic attachment.
HSE	"Train Derailment at Potters Bar 10 May 2002, Third Progress Report", 2002, Health and Safety Commission, Investigation Board, HSE Books, London: ORR. Cited: Potters Bar Inquiry. See electronic attachment.
HSE	"The Southall Rail Accident Inquiry Report", 2000, Health and Safety Commission led by John Uff HSE Books, London: ORR. Cited: Southall Inquiry. See electronic attachment.
HSE	"The Ladbroke Grove Rail Inquiry", 2001, Health and Safety Commission led by Prof. Cullen, HSE Books, London: ORR. Cited: Ladbroke Inquiry. See electronic attachment.
HSE	"Train Derailment at Hatfield" 2006, Health and Safety Commission, Investigation Board, HSE Books, London: ORR, Cited: Hatfield Inquiry. See electronic attachment.
Jescheck / Weigend, Hans-Heinrich / Thomas	"Lehrbuch des Strafrechts: Allgemeiner Teil", 1996, 5th Ed., Duncker & Humblot Berlin, Cited: Lehrbuch des Strafrechts AT.

Keenan, Denis	"English Law", 2007, 15th Ed., Pearson Longman London.
Keenan, Denis	"Company Law" 2005, 13th Ed., Pearson Longman London.
Law Commission	"Criminal Law: Involuntary Manslaughter, Consultation Paper No. 135", 1996, London: HSMO, Cited: Consultation Paper 135.
Law Commission	"Legislating the Criminal Code: Involuntary Manslaughter, Item 11 of the Sixth Programme of Law Reform: Criminal Law, Report No. 237", 1996, London: HSMO, Cited: Report 237. See electronic attachment.
Möllering, Jürgen	"Zehn Thesen zur Strafbarkeit von juristischen Personen und Personenmehrheiten", 2002, in Strafrechtswissenschaft und Strafrechtspolitik, Vol. 4 Reform des Sanktionenrechts: Verbandsstrafe, pp. 71-75, Hettinger (Publisher), Nomos Verlagsgesellschaft Baden-Baden.
Peck, Miriam / Brevitt, Brenda,	"The Corporate Manslaughter and Corporate Homicide Bill, Research Paper 06/46", 2006, House of Commons Library, Cited: Peck / Brevitt. See electronic attachment.
Schönke / Schröder,	"Kommentar zum StGB", 2006, 27th Ed., C. H. Beck München, Cited: Schönke / Schröder / Editor
Schroth, Hans- Jürgen	"Unternehmen als Normadressaten und Sanktionssubjekte", 1993, Giessener Rechtswissenschaftliche Abhandlungen Vol. 7, Brühlscher Verlag Gießen, Cited: Unternehmen als Normadressaten.
Senge, Lothar	"Karlsruher Kommentar zum Gesetz über Ordnungswidrigkeiten", 2000, 3rd Edition, C. H. Beck München, Cited: Senge / Editor.
Slapper, Gary	"A corporate killing", 1994, in NLJ Practitioner, p. 1735.
Slapper, Gary	"Corporate Manslaughter: The Changing Legal Scenery", See electronic attachment.
Tiedemann, Klaus	"Die Bebußung von Unternehmen nach dem 2. Gesetz zur Bekämpfung der Wirtschaftskriminalität", 1988, in NJW, pp. 1169-1177.

Watkins, Ian	"Much Ado About Nothing (The Corporate Manslaughter Bill)", 2005, in Justice of the Peace, pp. 488-492.
Wells, Celia	"The Corporate Manslaughter Proposals: Pragmatism, Paradox and Peninsularity", 1996, in Crim.L.R., pp. 545-553.
Wells, Celia	"Corporate Manslaughter: A Cultural and Legal Form", 1997, in Crim.L.F., Vol. 6, No. 1, pp. 45-72.

Lightning Source UK Ltd.
Milton Keynes UK
29 December 2010

164966UK00006B/25/P

9 783836 496254